Happy 100th Day!

Written by Kristen Avery
Illustrated by Maureen Ivy Fisher

Celebration Press
An Imprint of Pearson Learning

I have one hundred buttons.

I have one hundred pennies.

I have one hundred stamps.

I have one hundred marbles.

I have one hundred stickers.

I have one hundred links.

We have one hundred candles.